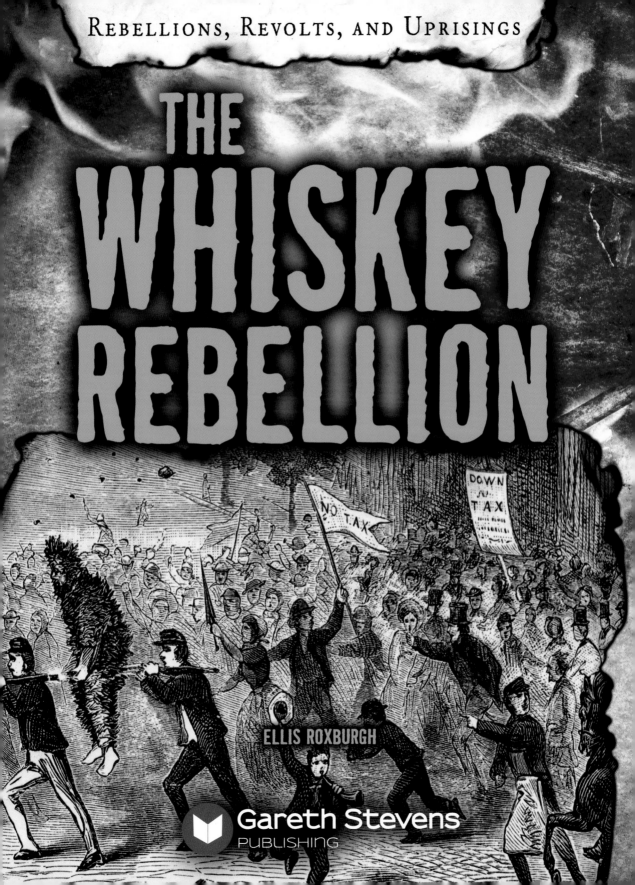

THE WHISKEY REBELLION

ELLIS ROXBURGH

Gareth Stevens
PUBLISHING

Please visit our website, www.garethstevens.com. For a free color catalog of all our high-quality books, call toll-free 1-800-542-2595 or fax 1-877-542-2596.

CATALOGING-IN-PUBLICATION DATA

Names: Roxburgh, Ellis.
Title: The Whiskey Rebellion / Ellis Roxburgh.
Description: New York : Gareth Stevens Publishing, 2018. | Series: Rebellions, revolts, and uprisings | Includes index.
Identifiers: ISBN 9781538207710 (pbk.) | ISBN 9781538207697 (library bound) | ISBN 9781538207574 (6 pack)
Subjects: LCSH: Whiskey Rebellion, Pa., 1794--Juvenile literature.
Classification: LCC E315.R69 2018 | DDC 973.4'3--dc23

Published in 2018 by
Gareth Stevens Publishing
111 East 14th Street, Suite 349
New York, NY 10003

Copyright © 2018 Gareth Stevens Publishing

For Brown Bear Books Ltd:
Managing Editor: Tim Cooke
Designer: Lynne Lennon
Editorial Director: Lindsey Lowe
Children's Publisher: Anne O'Daly
Design Manager: Keith Davis
Picture Manager: Sophie Mortimer

Picture Credits
Cover: Getty: Three Lions / Stringer
Interior: 123rf: 5, 18, 25; Alamy: Granger Historical Picture Archive 34, 38, 42, North Wind Picture Archives 26; Bridgeman Art Library: 24; Dreamstime: 39; istockphoto: 13, 35; Library of Congress: 6, 7, 9, 20, 23, 28, 29, 31, 32, 43; Metropolitan Museum of Art: 4, 33, Gift of Frederic W. Steven 17; Courtesy Mount Vernon: 40, 41; Public Domain: 10, Cincinnati Art Museum 12, Dickinson College Archives and Special Collections 16, NMM 14, University of Pennsylvania 22, U.S. Treasury 36, U.S. Treasury Bureau of Engraving and Printing 37; Seth Kaller Historic Documents & Legacy Collections: 30; Shutterstock: 21, Everett Historical 11, 15; Thinkstock: istockphoto 68, 19; U.S. Federal Government: 27.

All other images Brown Bear Books

Brown Bear Books has made every attempt to contact the copyright holder.
If anyone has any information please contact licensing@brownbearbooks.co.uk

Manufactured in the United States of America

CPSIA compliance information: Batch #CS17GS. For further information contact Gareth Stevens, New York, New York at 1-800-542-2595.

CONTENTS

WORDS IN THE GLOSSARY APPEAR IN **BOLD** TYPE THE FIRST TIME THEY ARE USED IN THE TEXT.

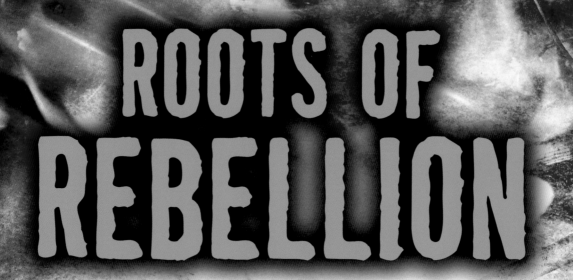

ROOTS OF REBELLION

After independence from Britain was declared in 1776, the new government of the United States faced rebellion from its own citizens. The rebellion was the first serious challenge to the new country.

George Washington (standing, left) leads troops across the Delaware River during the Revolutionary War (1775–1783).

The Treaty of Paris formally ended the Revolutionary War in 1783. The United States had gained independence from Great Britain and the new country began to set up its own government.

The Revolutionary War had been very expensive. The new United States had taken over the debts run up by the former **colonies** fighting the British. In winter 1791, the US Congress approved a bill to tax all **distilled spirits**. This included whiskey, which was then the most popular alcoholic spirit. The tax was the idea of the first Secretary of the Treasury, Alexander Hamilton. He wanted to raise money to start reducing the US national debt.

Hamilton's Federal Excise Tax soon became known as the "whiskey tax."

The Protestors

The proposed tax was the first US tax to be imposed on a homegrown product, and many Americans did not think the new tax was fair. They included many veterans of the war against the British. The objectors to the new tax claimed that it went against the principles of the revolution. One of the main causes of the Revolutionary War had been the people's anger at being taxed without having representation in the British parliament that had imposed the taxes.

First Secretary of the Treasury

Alexander Hamilton (c.1755–1804) was born in the West Indies. He was orphaned at an early age and was sent to North America for an education. Hamilton played a key role in the Revolutionary War, where he fought alongside George Washington. After the war, Hamilton became Washington's first Secretary of the Treasury. He set the nation's economic policies, including founding a national bank. Hamilton died in a duel against his political rival, Aaron Burr.

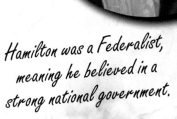

Hamilton was a Federalist, meaning he believed in a strong national government.

An Unfair Tax

Hamilton's excise bill proposed taxing people who distilled whiskey according to the amount they produced. Large-scale producers paid tax at the rate of 6 cents a gallon, but small-scale producers had to pay tax at a higher rate of 9 cents a gallon. The more whiskey a producer distilled, the lower the rate of tax he or she paid. At the time, many farmers produced their own whiskey on a small scale. They objected to having to pay the higher rate of tax. These small producers also objected to the the demand that the tax had to be paid in cash.

No Taxation without Representation

"No taxation without representation" became a rallying cry of the Revolutionary War. The British government taxed American colonists, but it did not allow them to elect representatives to sit in the British Parliament. As Britain increased taxes in the American colonies to pay for its wars in Europe, the colonists resented the increased financial burden.

This cartoon shows the "funeral" of the Stamp Act, another unpopular tax that Americans forced Britain to withdraw.

The Producers

In the 1700s, many farmers used their spare grain and corn to make liquor, which they could sell or exchange for other goods. In western Pennsylvania, farmers relied on selling liquor. They could not easily transport grain to sell in towns to the east because the Allegheny Mountains were in the way. The **packhorses** that crossed the mountains could only carry a limited amount of grain. By turning the grain to alcohol, farmers could transport a larger volume across the mountains and then sell it for more money.

Western Pennsylvania was cut off from the east by the Allegheny Mountains.

The farmers were already angry with the government. At the time, western Pennsylvania was on the **frontier** of the United States. As **pioneers** moved west, they came under attack from Native Americans. People on the frontier were angry that the government had failed to do anything to stop these attacks. Now, however, they felt that the government was becoming unnecessarily involved in their business.

Organized Resistance

In July 1791, a group of farmers and politicians met at Redstone Old Fort, on a Native American trail on the eastern bank of the Monongahela River in Pennsylvania. The meeting was the first act of what became the Whiskey Rebellion.

Distilling Spirits

When they used grain to make spirits, the farmers of Pennsylvania were following a long tradition. People began distilling spirits many centuries ago by mashing grain, allowing it to ferment in water, then distilling the liquid. The ancient Chinese were distilling a drink from rice beer by 800 bc. The Arabs also learned to make a distilled drink from wine. When the Arabs conquered part of Spain, they introduced distillation to Europe. From Europe, settlers later took it to the Americas.

Native Americans sometimes attacked white settlers on the frontier who tried to take their land for farming.

Forts such as Fort Ligonier were built throughout western Pennsylvania.

The men who gathered at Redstone Old Fort in 1791 all agreed that they would not pay the new whiskey tax. They also agreed to try to stop tax collectors from collecting the money from other taxes. Some of the farmers thought that they should use violence against the officials if necessary.

Escalating Violence

In the months following the meeting, farmers in several counties in western Pennsylvania threatened violence to prevent federal officers from collecting the hated whiskey tax. Some tax collectors were outsiders, but in some communities local men had taken on the job. This did not protect them from their neighbors' anger.

DID YOU KNOW?

BEING COVERED IN TAR AND FEATHERS HAS A LONG
HISTORY OF BEING USED AS A PUNISHMENT. IT WAS FIRST
RECORDED IN ENGLAND IN THE 1100s.

On September 11, 1791, a tax collector named Robert Johnson tried to collect taxes in Washington County. Farmers poured hot tar over him and covered him with feathers that stuck to the tar. The same thing happened to the man who was sent to serve **warrants** on Johnson's attackers. As a result, the collection of the new tax was abandoned in 1791 and early 1792.

Farmers tar and feather a tax collector during the Whiskey Rebellion.

WHO WERE THE REBELS?

The people who opposed the whiskey tax were mainly poor frontiersmen and farmers who felt badly treated by the new government.

Life for pioneers in western Pennsylvania had grown worse after the end of the Revolutionary War. Wealthy landlords, who often lived on the East Coast, began to buy the land. Land prices rose, and fewer settlers could afford them. By 1795, 60 percent of settlers did not own any land. The situation was worst in Fayette County, where very few of the settlers owned land.

→

Most settlers on the frontier were poor farming families.

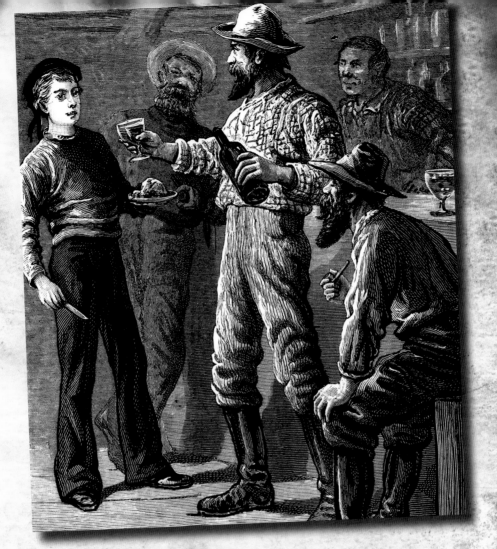

Alcoholic spirits were popular among frontier settlers. ↑

A Hard Life

Living standards for most families were falling. Farmers lived in mud-floored, flea-ridden cabins that filled up with thick smoke from the fire because most homes did not have a chimney. Food was scarce. One of the few pleasures farmers had was drinking the liquor they made from grain. Many farmers had their own **stills** to make whiskey. In 1791, Washington County had one still for every 20 to 30 families.

PATRIOTIC WHISKEY

BEFORE THE REVOLUTIONARY WAR, RUM WAS THE MOST POPULAR ALCOHOLIC DRINK IN NORTH AMERICA. DURING THE WAR, HOWEVER, THE BRITISH BLOCKADED AMERICAN PORTS. IT BECAME IMPOSSIBLE TO IMPORT THE SUGAR NEEDED TO MAKE RUM. NEW ENGLAND RUM DISTILLERS INSTEAD BEGAN TO MAKE WHISKEY FROM RYE. THEY PROMOTED WHISKEY AS AN ALL-AMERICAN DRINK MADE FROM HOMEGROWN AMERICAN GRAIN.

British warships blockaded American ports during the war.

The Many Uses for Whiskey

Farmers did not drink all the whiskey they produced. They used liquor to pay for labor. It was hard to find casual workers, and most men would only work in return for whiskey. When the whiskey ran out, the workers moved on. Farmers also sold whiskey to the US Army. The army paid cash, making whiskey one of the farmers' few sources of reliable **revenue**. The liquor was also a popular item to **barter**.

Unlikely Rebels

The farmers who took a stand against the whiskey tax were unusual rebels. Many of them were poor veteran soldiers who had fought against the British in the Revolutionary War. Now they were trying to make a living as farmers on the newly opened frontier. Life was hard. The government had encouraged settlers to move to the frontier, but those who did so felt let down that the new government had not helped them fight off Native American attacks. Many settlers resented paying tax when it seemed that little of the money the tax raised would be spent on the frontier.

Farmers on the frontier cleared the wilderness to create space to grow their crops.

The Moderate Rebels

The Whiskey Rebellion, which lasted from 1791 to 1794, was initially led by men with **moderate** views about the new government. They did not want to use violence to resist the tax. They believed that they should convince the government to cancel the tax. These leaders of the rebellion came from the more wealthy and educated parts of frontier society. Colonel Edward Cook (1738–1808) of Fayette County was a respected member of the community in western Pennsylvania. He was a landowner, lawyer, and politician who had served as a member of the Provincial Congress in Philadelphia in 1776. Although Cook was a moderate, he supported the rebels and was elected as chairman for several key meetings, including the original meeting held at the Redstone Old Fort in July 1791.

Moderate Men

Like Edward Cook, the politicians Hugh Henry Brackenridge of Pittsburgh and Albert Gallatin of Fayette County also opposed the whiskey tax but they did not support the use of violence

Hugh Henry Brackenridge tried to persuade the rebels not to use violence.

16

→

Albert Gallatin later regretted his role in the Whiskey Rebellion, which he called his "only political sin."

to protest against it.

Hugh Henry Brackenridge (1748–1816) was one of the leading politicians of Pittsburgh. Later in his life, Brackenridge became a justice on the Supreme Court of Pennsylvania. At the time, he felt he should help the frontier farmers against the government because he believed that the whiskey tax was unfair.

Albert Gallatin (1761–1849) was also a politician. He later became the longest serving US Secretary of the Treasury, serving between 1801 and 1814. Born in Switzerland, Gallatin settled in western Pennsylvania after he emigrated to the United States. He had opposed the whiskey tax in the US Congress. Gallatin attended protest meetings in Pennsylvania but advised the protestors to stay within the law.

More Radical Leaders

Other rebel leaders took a more **radical** approach. They included the lawyer David Bradford (1762–1808) and the popular preacher Herman Husband (1724–1795). Both of them became wanted men for their roles in the rebellion.

17

BRADFORD'S ESCAPE

DAVID BRADFORD'S ESCAPE AT THE END OF THE WHISKEY REBELLION BECAME FAMOUS. THE STORY WAS THAT HE JUMPED OUT OF A WINDOW IN THE MIDDLE OF THE NIGHT ONTO A WAITING HORSE AND GALLOPED OFF TO HIS FREEDOM. THE TRUTH WAS MORE ORDINARY. BRADFORD TRAVELED INTO PITTSBURGH, FROM WHERE HE TOOK A COAL BARGE DOWN THE MISSISSIPPI RIVER TO BEGIN A NEW LIFE IN LOUISIANA.

David Bradford defended farmers' rights to make whiskey without being taxed.

The government offered rewards for their capture.

David Bradford was a lawyer from Washington County. He joined in attacks on tax collectors, and the government saw him as a ringleader of the rebellion. When federal cavalry came to arrest him on October 25, 1794, Bradford fled to Louisiana, which was then in Spanish hands. He was eventually pardoned by President John Adams in March 1799.

Herman Husband was a revolutionary Quaker preacher who had made a name for fighting against **corrupt** colonial officials. He was outspoken in his support of local democracy. Husband had taken part in the Regulator Rebellion in North Carolina between 1765 and 1771. He did not support violence, but Gallatin nicknamed him the "Pennsylvania madman" for his fiery speaking style. Husband became a target for the US government. He was one of the first rebels to be arrested in October 1794, but he died the following year, after charges against him had been dismissed.

Separated by the Allegheny Mountains, the rebels felt far removed from decisions made on the East Coast.

19

REBELLION!

The people of western Pennsylvania spent 4 years resisting government attempts to collect taxes. The dispute reached its peak in 1794.

After the first meeting at Redstone Old Fort on July 27, 1791, the farmers and their supporters agreed to hold a **convention** in Pittsburgh in September. The convention was attended by many moderates. They appealed to the Pennsylvania Assembly and the US House of Representatives for help against the tax. In May 1792, the whiskey tax was lowered by 1 cent per gallon.

Most of the rebels lived in isolated homesteads on the frontier.

The farmers used any surplus rye to make their own whiskey.

Meanwhile, farmers in west Pennsylvania had turned to violence. They had attacked the first tax collector to arrive in the area. They also attacked other tax collectors and people suspected of being government supporters. Attackers beat, tarred, and feathered their victims. They robbed them and **branded** them with hot irons before releasing them.

Violence Resumes

There was a lull in attacks as moderates organized meetings to **petition** the government. They achieved the reduction in the tax. Then, in the summer of 1792, the violent protests started up again. A tax collector named William Faulkner was threatened and told not to use his home in Washington County as an excise office to collect taxes. Faulkner agreed to the demands, but not before his home had been attacked.

The protests against the whiskey tax were now led by a group that called itself the Mingo Creek Association. They held another convention in Pittsburgh in August 1792. The association argued that the rebels should use violence to make their point. The moderates argued against them.

Hamilton Intervenes

After the attack on Faulkner's house and the second Pittsburgh convention, Alexander Hamilton sent the politician George Clymer (1793–1813) to western Pennsylvania to find out what was happening. Clymer reported that some counties were refusing outright to pay the tax, particularly Washington County. Even the counties Clymer said would pay the tax, such as Fayette County, were experiencing high levels of violence.

The government saw the unrest as a threat to the rule of law. Alexander Hamilton wrote a **proclamation** that criticized anyone who refused to pay the tax. The proclamation was signed by President George Washington.

George Clymer was appointed head of tax collection in Pennsylvania.

DID YOU KNOW?

GEORGE CLYMER WAS ONE OF THE FIRST PEOPLE TO ARGUE THAT AMERICA SHOULD BE INDEPENDENT OF BRITAIN. HE SIGNED THE DECLARATION OF INDEPENDENCE IN 1776.

Washington offered a reward for the capture of any attackers, but none were identified or caught. Attacks on government officials continued through 1793 and into 1794.

In March 1794, officials in Fayette Country tried to make collection of the tax more acceptable to the protestors. They replaced all tax collectors in the area with "respectable" men they hoped would command respect from their neighbors. The protestors were already divided, but the new development split moderates such as Albert Gallatin and Hugh Henry Brackenridge entirely from the Mingo Creek Association. The poor farmers of the association felt they were left little choice but to resort to greater violence.

A Reign of Terror

By the summer of 1794, rebels in Washington County regarded any farmer who did not oppose the whiskey tax as a **traitor**. Rebels destroyed the stills of anyone they suspected of sympathy with the government.

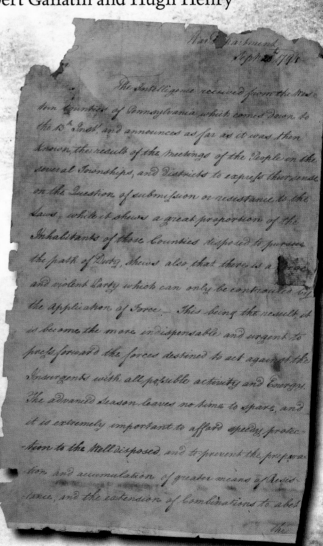

→

This letter from Alexander Hamilton includes reports of the rebellion in Pennsylvania.

23

Unknown Author

"Tom the Tinker" wrote a series of letters about the rebel cause that threatened violence against those who opposed the rebels. His true identity was never revealed, but experts believe he may have been the rebel named John Holcroft. Some rebel groups called themselves "Tom the Tinker's Men." However, Tom's threats were never carried out.

The new leader of the rebels was a farmer and distiller named John Holcroft (1741–1816). He had taken part in the Shays' Rebellion in Massachusetts in 1786 and 1787 against tax and debt collection. Holcroft called the attacks on other farmers in Washington County "mending the stills."

This illustration shows an illegal whiskey still during the height of the rebellion in 1794.

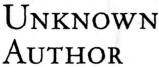

The Violence Continues

On June 22, 1794, US Marshal David Lenox left Philadelphia for western Pennsylvania. His job was to serve **writs** against people who had not paid their taxes. All went smoothly until he rode into Monongahela to serve the last few writs.

Lennox was with the local tax inspector, General John Neville. Neville was a prominent landowner and slaveowner who also owned the largest whiskey distillery in the area. Until he had been made a government inspector, Neville had been a strong opponent to the tax. His change of heart angered many local people.

When Neville and Lenox came to the farm of William Miller, Miller refused to accept the writ.

Pennsylvanians on both sides of the rebellion continued to distill their own whiskey.

A group of rebels turned up and a scuffle broke out. A shot was fired. Although no one was injured, news of the violent incident soon spread. The two government men fled as more angry rebels gathered.

25

A Revenue Inspector

John Neville (1731–1803) had played an important role in the Revolutionary War. As a result, he was promoted to brigadier general in September 1783. Neville was very wealthy and owned one of the biggest houses in western Pennsylvania where he served as a revenue inspector. Neville's attempts to collect the whiskey tax made him very unpopular among local people.

Neville and Marshal Lennox attempt to collect taxes at William Miller's farm.

Neville was a veteran of the Revolutionary War.

Taking Revenge

Led by John Holcroft, the rebels headed for John Neville's home at Bower Hill. When they arrived, shots were fired and several people were wounded. William Miller's nephew, Oliver Miller, died from his wounds. The local community was outraged. The next day, July 16, 1794, Major James McFarlane, another veteran of the Revolutionary War, led 600 rebels to Neville's house, which was guarded by 10 soldiers. The two sides exchanged fire, and McFarlane was shot and killed. Furious, the rebels set fire to Neville's barn, the slave quarters, and the mansion itself, which burned down. Disguised as a woman, Neville escaped with his family.

FIGHTING AUTHORITY

The destruction of General Neville's home forced President George Washington into action. The government in Philadelphia was worried the rebellion was getting out of hand.

After the death of Major McFarlane, the opponents of the whiskey tax met on July 21, 1794, to decide on their next steps. Hugh Henry Brackenridge suggested the rebels should ask for a meeting with President Washington. He argued that the attack on John Neville's home had been an act of **high treason**.

→ George Washington saw the rebellion as a direct challenge to the authority of the government.

David Bradford's supporters gathered at Braddock's Field.

Brackenridge feared the government would send troops to put down future rebellions. He said, "what has been done might be **morally** right but it was legally wrong."

Brackenridge was opposed by David Bradford. Bradford suspected that local people in Pittsburgh were sending information to the goverment. Bradford arranged for his supporters to intercept the federal mail as it was carried from Pittsburgh to Washington, DC. He wanted to find out who in the city was supporting the government.

Braddock's Field

On July 30, 1794, Bradford summoned 7,000 rebels to Braddock's Field, 8 miles (13 km) from Pittsburgh. Rumors spread that they were going to burn Pittsburgh down.

Fear gripped the town. Bradford now began to negotiate with officials from Pittsburgh. He demanded that all tax collectors be removed from the city. The officials agreed to **banish** citizens who had written letters criticizing the rebels. In return, Brackenridge persuaded the rebels to stage a small protest march through the city.

Washington Acts

On August 7, President Washington issued a proclamation. In it, he summarized what had been happening in western Pennsylvania for the past 3 years. He also announced that he would call out the **militia** to stop any treasonable activity in the region.

In western Pennsylvania, rebels from the counties that were most affected by the rebellion met again on August 14 at Parkinson's Ferry, which lay on the west bank of the Monongahela River at the mouth of Pigeon Creek.

THE NORWICH PACKET.

PRINTED BY JOHN TRUMBULL—NORWICH.

[—VOL. XXI.—]   THURSDAY, OCTOBER 9, 1794.   [—No. 1073.—]

Washington's proclamation about the rebellion was printed in local newspapers.

The rebels chose the location for its central position, because all the roads met there. The rebels met at a spot overlooking the river, which is still known as "Whiskey Point."

Moderate rebels, such as Albert Gallatin and Hugh Henry Brackenridge, were dismayed to read Washington's proclamation. They decided that the best course of action was to give in, but they were outvoted by others such as the preacher Herman Husband, who wanted to carry on the protests. The rebels did, however, agree to send representatives to meet with peace commissioners sent to Pennsylvania by President Washington.

The Army Is Sent In

By now, however, Washington's patience had run out. He could see that the dispute might continue **indefinitely**. Although he had sent peace commissioners, he also called up the militia. State governors raised troops in Pennsylvania, New Jersey, Maryland, and Virginia to be sent to western Pennsylvania. Washington himself rode out to inspect the 12,950 troops who gathered for the task.

←

The radical rebels argued that they were fighting for the same principles that inspired the Revolutionary War.

LIGHT-HORSE HARRY

GENERAL HENRY LEE (1756–1818) EARNED THE NICKNAME "LIGHT-HORSE HARRY" DURING THE REVOLUTIONARY WAR. HE COMMANDED A LIGHT CAVALRY UNIT. AFTER THE WAR, HE SERVED AS THE GOVERNOR OF VIRGINIA. HE SPOKE AT THE FUNERAL OF GEORGE WASHINGTON ON DECEMBER 26, 1799, WHEN HE DESCRIBED THE PRESIDENT AS "FIRST IN WAR, FIRST IN PEACE, AND FIRST IN THE HEARTS OF HIS COUNTRYMEN." LEE WAS THE FATHER OF ROBERT E. LEE WHO LED THE CONFEDERATE ARMY DURING THE CIVIL WAR (1861-1865).

Washington believed that such a large force would scare the rebels into surrender. He put the militia under the command of General Henry Lee, governor of Virginia. Alexander Hamilton, who had urged Washington to stop the rebellion with force, traveled with the army as an advisor.

This was the home of "Light-Horse Harry" Lee.

32

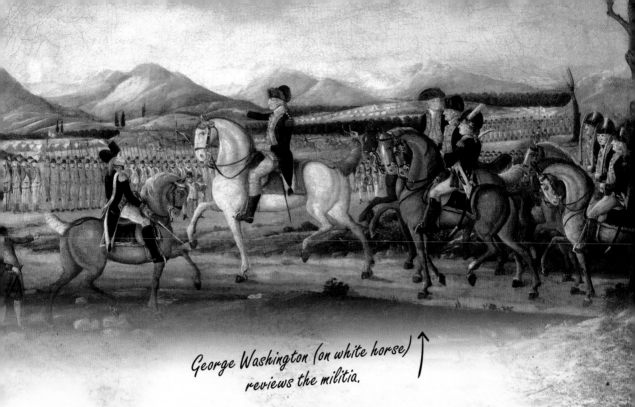

George Washington (on white horse) reviews the militia.

A Forceful Arrival

Lee's militia had a difficult journey to western Pennsylvania. Rainy weather caused many creeks to flood. There were not enough provisions, and 116 soldiers became too sick to be able to continue. Eventually, however, the army arrived at different locations throughout western Pennsylvania.

Its arrival had the desired effect. By the time the rebels met again at Parkinson's Ferry on October 24, David Bradford and the other radical leaders who had supported armed rebellion had disappeared. The prospect of fighting the army had been enough to scare them off.

DID YOU KNOW?

GEORGE WASHINGTON COULD ONLY RAISE A FEDERAL MILITIA AFTER A JUDGE RULED THAT AUTHORITIES IN PENNSYLVANIA COULD NOT STOP THE REBELLION.

The President and the Rebellion

When the Whiskey Rebellion broke out in 1791, George Washington was finishing his first term as the country's first president. He was unanimously re-elected for a second term by the electoral college in 1792. In 1794, when he decided to act against the rebels, the US Army was too small to send to western Pennsylvania. Before the militia headed into the field, Washington went out to review them in the field. He is the only sitting president and commander in chief to have done so.

To help the remaining rebels save face and to claim that they had presented their grievances to the government, Alexander Hamilton suggested that representatives of the rebels should meet with General Lee. At the meeting, the rebels argued against the tax and defended their actions.

Lee listened politely to the arguments. The next day, however, he wrote to them rejecting their version of events. Lee made it clear that he felt the local people had been involved in treason.

Alexander Hamilton, himself a veteran of the Revolutionary War, accompanied the militia as a civilian.

Lee also argued that the rebels had only backed down when the army arrived. The rebellion had been a serious challenge to federal authority.

The army arrested around 40 rebels, who were taken to Philadelphia to stand trial. They included the preacher Herman Husband. Bradford and other radicals had fled westward. Less than 3 weeks after the militia had arrived in western Pennsylvania, it began to withdraw. On November 19, 1794, the Whiskey Rebellion was at an end.

Whiskey remained popular in the United States throughout the 1800s. ↓

DEFEAT AND LEGACY

After George Washington sent in the militia, the long rebellion quickly collapsed in the face of federal power. The effect of the rebellion, however, is still felt today.

The US Treasury Building is in Washington, DC. Alexander Hamilton was determined to enforce the Treasury's demands.

The Whiskey Rebellion marked an important point in the development of the young United States. The 13 colonies had gone to war with their British rulers over the question of taxation without representation. Barely 20 years after the colonies had declared their independence, the issue had been raised again.

In 1800, the former rebel Albert Gallatin became secretary of the treasury.

The End of the Rebellion

When the federal army withdrew from western Pennsylvania in November 1794, around 20 rebels had been imprisoned. George Washington had to decide whether he should make an example of them or whether he should show them **clemency** in the interests of national unity.

The prisoners were marched to Philadelphia to stand trial. However, some of them were released before going on trial, and of the 12 men who did appear in court, only two were found guilty. There was not enough evidence to **convict** and imprison the captured men.

Shays' Rebellion

One reason George Washington was eager to put down the whiskey rebellion was because it followed Shays' Rebellion. During 1786 and 1787, farmers led an armed uprising in Massachusetts against what they saw as unjust tax demands. Shays' Rebellion had brought Washington out of retirement to become president. He wanted to avoid a similar uprising.

Opponents and supporters of Shays' Rebellion fight in Massachusetts.

Alexander Hamilton had hoped to see Albert Gallatin and others hang for their part in the rebellion. In fact, these moderates had tried to control David Bradford and the more violent rebel leaders. The juries in Philadelphia seemed to judge that all the people of western Pennsylvania had been responsible for the rebellion, not just the handful of leaders who appeared in court.

Not Guilty

The Quaker preacher Herman Husband was taken into custody after the rebellion, but he was not tried for treason like the other rebels. Husband was tried for sedition, or encouraging people to revolt. The jury found him not guilty. He was released on May 12, 1795. By then his health was destroyed, and he died the following month from pneumonia.

The courthouse in Philadelphia. Husband and the others were taken to the city to stand trial.

The court found two men guilty. One was Philip Wigle, who had beaten up the tax collector Benjamin Wells. The other, John Mitchell, was a mentally impaired man whom David Bradford had sent to rob the mail. Wigle and Mitchell were sentenced to death, but with the crisis over, Washington **pardoned** them. It was already 6 months since the army had left western Pennsylvania, and dragging out the process further was preventing the country from moving on.

Life Goes On

In western Pennsylvania, meanwhile, General Lee had issued a general pardon. The population had sworn oaths of loyalty to the United States. The tax collectors went back to work, and many more whiskey stills had been officially registered.

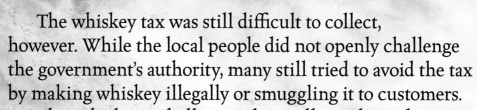

The whiskey tax was still difficult to collect, however. While the local people did not openly challenge the government's authority, many still tried to avoid the tax by making whiskey illegally or smuggling it to customers.

The Whiskey Rebellion took its toll on Alexander Hamilton. He retired from the cabinet and his position as secretary of the treasury early in 1795. Modern historians see Hamilton's determination to defeat the whiskey rebels as a low point in what was generally a remarkable career.

This barrel of whiskey was made at George Washington's distillery.

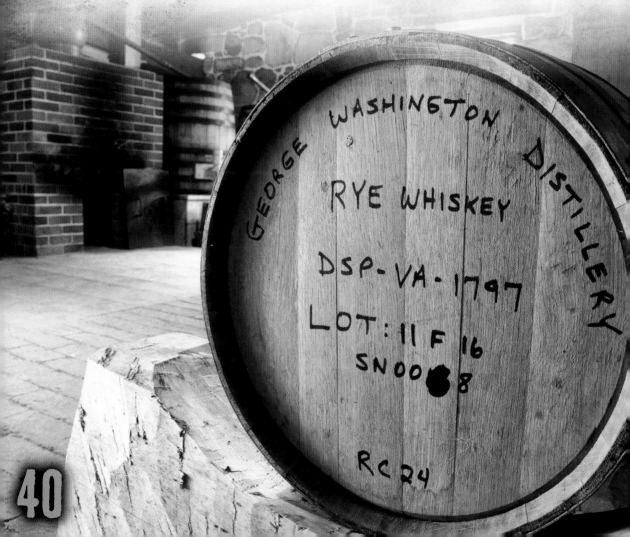

GEORGE WASHINGTON DISTILLERY

RYE WHISKEY

DSP-VA-1797

LOT: 11 F 16

SN 00 8

RC 24

Washington's Whiskey

By the time of his death in 1799, George Washington had become the largest whiskey producer in the United States. Only 2 years earlier, the farm manager at Washington's estate, Mount Vernon, encouraged him to go into the whiskey business. From the start, the whiskey made a good profit and the business expanded rapidly. In 1799, Mount Vernon produced about 11,000 gallons (42,000 L) of whiskey.

The distillery at Mount Vernon is still in use today.

The Legacy

The Whiskey Rebellion had taken place because of disputes about the level of interference by the federal government in people's lives. The poor farmers of western Pennsylvania felt their lives were far removed from the lives of people on the East Coast. Their remote location and the barrier of the Allegheny Mountains meant that many did not feel as though they even lived in the same country as the eastern colonies.

The reluctance of the federal government to send the army to put down the many Native American attacks also made them angry.

Federal Power

President Washington realized from the start that the Whiskey Rebellion was about more than just whiskey. It was about the limits of federal power. For this reason, he saw the rebellion as a chance to impose the will of the federal government and to demonstrate its power over the whole emerging nation.

By the time the Whiskey Rebellion was over, it had cost the government almost $700,000, a huge sum at the time. Washington had raised an army as large as many of those that fought in the Revolutionary War. But the federal government had asserted its control over the lives of the American people.

The rebels were forced to signed this oath of allegiance to the United States.

The so-called Federalists, politicians who believed that the federal government should have more power relative to the power of the states, had strengthened their hold on politics. The rebellion had also set a **precedent** for sending in the military to put down uprisings.

The Act Is Repealed

The whiskey tax itself was short-lived. In 1800, Thomas Jefferson was elected the third president of the United States. His secretary of the treasury was the former rebel Albert Gallatin, who later called the Whiskey Rebellion his "only political sin." In 1802, the Federal Excise Tax, or whiskey tax, was **repealed**.

Thomas Jefferson repealed the unpopular whiskey tax in 1802.

TIMELINE

1791 **March:** The Excise Tax, also known as the "whiskey tax," becomes law.

July 27: Representatives of counties in western Pennsylvania meet at Redstone Old Fort to plan resistance to the tax.

September 7: Opponents of the tax meet at a convention in Pittsburgh.

September 11: A disguised gang tar and feather the tax collector Robert Johnson in Washington County.

1792 **May:** The tax on whiskey is lowered by 1 cent per gallon.

August: William Faulkner is threatened for allowing his home to be used as an excise [tax] office.

August 21: Opponents of the tax hold a second convention in Pittsburgh.

August: George Clymer visits western Pennsylvania and reports to the government that the situation is worse than they had thought.

September 15: George Washington issues a proclamation drafted by Alexander Hamilton that condemns opposition to the excise act.

1793 **November 22:** Armed men break into the home of tax collector Benjamin Wells of Lafayette County and force him to give up his job.

1794

March: Tax collectors are replaced by local men to try to make tax collection more acceptable.

July 15: When Marshal David Lenox and John Neville try to collect the tax at the home of William Miller, there is an exchange of gunfire.

July 16: A crowd attacks the home of John Neville, burning it down.

July 21: At a meeting of the rebels at Whiskey Point, Hugh Henry Brackenridge suggests asking for talks with the president.

July 26: Rebel David Bradford asks his supporters to rob the US mail. They find letters highly critical of the rebellion.

July 30: Bradford calls 7,000 supporters to Braddock's Field, where he threatens to march on Pittsburgh, but townspeople diffuse the threat.

August 7: George Washington announces his decision to send a federal militia force to western Pennsylvania.

October 3: George Washington reviews the militia on its way to Pennsylvania.

October: After a difficult march, the army arrives in western Pennsylvania.

October 24: When another rebel convention meets, all the radicals such as David Bradford have fled.

November 19: The US militia begins to leave western Pennsylvania.

1802

April 6: The whiskey tax is repealed.

GLOSSARY

banish: To send someone away from a place as a punishment.

barter: To trade by swapping goods for other goods or services.

branded: Permanently marked with a hot piece of metal.

clemency: Mercy.

colonies: Regions that are governed by another country.

convention: A large, formal meeting about a specific subject.

convict: To find someone guilty of a crime.

corrupt: Describes someone who acts dishonestly in return for personal gain.

distilled spirits: Alcoholic drinks that are made by distilling, or purifying, fermented juice from plants such as grains.

frontier: The edge of settlement next to the uninhabited wilderness.

high treason: The crime of betraying one's country.

indefinitely: For an unlimited time.

militia: Citizens who act as a military force in times of emergency.

moderate: Avoiding extremes of behavior. Also, people who hold moderate views.

morally: Related to the idea of good and bad behavior.

packhorses: Horses that carry loads.

pardon: The act of forgiving someone for an offense.

petition: A formal written request to the authorities about an issue.

pioneers: The first people to settle in a region.

precedent: An action that sets an example for the future.

proclamation: An announcement about an important subject.

radical: Someone who holds extreme views.

repealed: Describes a law that has been cancelled.

revenue: Income.

stills: Apparatus for distilling alcoholic drinks.

traitor: Someone who betrays something.

warrants: Documents authorizing someone to make arrests.

writs: Legal documents that tell people they will be appearing in court.

FURTHER INFORMATION

Books

Hennessey, Jonathan, and Justin Greenwood.
Alexander Hamilton: The Graphic History of an American Founding Father.
Berkeley, CA: Ten Speed Press, 2017.

Korman, Justine, and Ron Fontes.
George Washington: Soldier, Hero, President. New York: DK Readers, 2009.

Schiel, Katy.
The Whiskey Rebellion: An Early Challenge to America's New Government.
New York: Rosen Publishing Group, 2004.

Stanley, George.
The New Republic, 1763–1815. Primary Source History of the United States. Milwaukee: World Almanac Library, 2005.

Websites

www.socialstudies forkids. com/wwww/us/ whiskeyrebelliondef.htm
A page with an account of the Whiskey Rebellion.

www.american-historama. org/1790-1800-new-nation/ whiskey-rebellion.htm
This fact sheet about the Whiskey Rebellion can be downloaded and printed.

www.pbs.org/wgbh/amex/ duel/peopleevents/pande22. html
This page about the rebellion comes from a PBS site about Alexander Hamilton.

www.youtube.com/ watch?v=rCcEEMEODKE
A short documentary about George Washington's role in the Whiskey Rebellion.

Publisher's note to educators and parents: Our editors have carefully reviewed these websites to ensure that they are suitable for students. Many websites change frequently, however, and we cannot guarantee that a site's future contents will continue to meet our high standards of quality and educational value. Be advised that students should be closely supervised whenever they access the Internet.

INDEX